PARANORMAL SEEKERS™

TRACKING THE YETI

JENNA VALE AND
LAURA ANNE GILMAN

rosen publishing's rosen central®
New York

Published in 2019 by The Rosen Publishing Group, Inc.
29 East 21st Street, New York, NY 10010

First Edition

Library of Congress Cataloging-in-Publication Data

Names: Vale, Jenna, author. | Gilman, Laura Anne, author.
Title: Tracking the Yeti / Jenna Vale and Laura Anne Gilman.
Description: First Edition. | New York : Rosen Publishing, 2019. | Series: Paranormal seekers | Includes bibliographical references and index. | Audience: Grades 5–8.
Identifiers: LCCN 2018016177 | ISBN 9781499467260 (library bound) | ISBN 9781499467437 (pbk.)
Subjects: LCSH: Yeti—Juvenile literature.
Classification: LCC QL89.2.Y4 V35 2018 | DDC 001.944—dc23
LC record available at https://lccn.loc.gov/2018016177

Manufactured in the United States of America

CONTENTS

INTRODUCTION

Though North America has myths, campfire stories, and mysterious video footage of Bigfoot, the snowy Himalayan mountains of Asia are home to sightings and frozen footprints of the legendary Yeti. A short, apelike creature covered in white hair, the Yeti, also known as the Abominable Snowman, has been vexing explorers and locals alike for generations.

Even the origin of the word "Yeti" has been cause for conjecture, as it is attributed to several sources. Some claim the name comes from the Tibetan words *Yah*, meaning "rock," and *Teh*, meaning "animal," combining to form "rock animal," perhaps for the Yeti's resemblance to a huge, snow-covered boulder. Others say it comes from the word for "magical creature," which it must have seemed to be to the local peoples who live in the foothills of the Himalayas.

As a cryptid, or animal whose existence has not been confirmed, the Yeti has been the subject of much speculation, particularly because it hails from such a remote location. The Himalayas run along the border between India, Nepal, and Tibet and have been referred to as the Roof of the World for their unparalleled height. For many, this is a place so distant and ethereal that it seems not to be of this earth; for many others, it is a place of great spiritual significance. Although much of the land around these rough peaks is uninhabited,

The Himalayas stretch approximately 1,500 miles (2,400 kilometers) across Asia. They extend through Afghanistan, Bhutan, China, India, Nepal, and Pakistan and are actually made up of three parallel ranges.

there are also local mountain communities whose lives and culture are intertwined with the complex landscape around them.

As cold and unforgiving as the heights of peaks such as Mount Everest are, there are also incredibly rich, biodiverse areas in the foothills and valleys below. There are thousands of plant species, and many wild animals in the region as well, including tigers, leopards, deer, bears, goats, and wolves. Sometimes strange tracks are found in the snow, possibly made by bears—or perhaps by something else.

The search for the Yeti in this vital, sprawling environment over the past few centuries has been like trying to find the proverbial needle in a haystack. The journey has been thrilling, with a history of climbing mountains, smuggling artifacts, and testing DNA evidence, all of which have led to more questions than answers. Although the Yeti calls such a remote area of the world home, this cryptid has reached the public consciousness so effectively that it has become a recognizable figure in popular culture as well as an ever-elusive subject for explorers and scientists alike. The main driving question is: If the Yeti is real, what exactly is it?

CHAPTER ONE

HISTORY OF THE HIMALAYAS

Although the region around the Himalayan mountains is notoriously difficult to traverse and settle, it has still been subject to the migration of people and ideas. The earliest known treks through the area were made by shepherds, pilgrims, and traders, with recorded history dating back to 800 BCE, when the Kirat dynasty ruled Tibet. It was also during this time that Buddhism—brought from India by traveling monks, merchants, and scholars to the royal court—came to the foothills of the Himalayas. After 300 CE, more people traveled from neighboring India to Tibet. They brought with them a more modern culture of record keeping and the minting of money. They also brought the religion of Hinduism. Architecture and decorative arts such as sculpture flourished in the Himalayas as well.

In the thirteenth century, British traders and explorers arrived in China and India, and Western influences began to creep in. In 1600, the British East India Company was created to simplify trade with India. One hundred and fifty years later, the British East India Company had grown to the point where it was, in effect, running the day-to-day governance of India. But even then, with the British in charge, the Himalayas remained relatively untouched, both because they were too difficult to explore and because there was little in the region that was of financial interest to England.

Merchants crossed through frozen Himalayan passes for generations. They used mule caravans to reach cities such as Lhasa, China, to conduct business and engage in both commercial and cultural exchange.

THE SHERPA PEOPLE

Today, the inhabitants of the Himalayas are more connected to the rest of the world, thanks to modern means of communication. The region itself, however, still remains a place set apart, separated from the rest of the world by a combination of geography, politics, and climate. One local group there are the Sherpas, who originated in Tibet, having migrated over the mountains to Nepal about five centuries ago. Before it became known as the name of a distinct cultural group, the word "Sherpa" originally meant "people from the East."

The Sherpas were originally farmers, herders, and traders. When the Western explorers arrived, Sherpa hunters became their guides and earned a well-deserved worldwide reputation for their mountaineering abilities. Sherpa guides are mentioned in almost every historical account of attempts to climb Mount Everest, including the famous expedition in 1953 when New Zealand climber Sir Edmund Hillary and Sherpa mountaineer Tenzing Norgay became the first to reach the summit. The Sherpa mountaineer who has reached Mount Everest's summit more than any other

A climber and a Sherpa guide hang an offering of Buddhist prayer flags. As wind blows through the flags, it is believed that prayers and mantras spread across the countryside to benefit those who are nearby.

is Apa Sherpa, who has reached the mountaintop a record-breaking twenty-one times, with the latest climb completed in 2011.

It was from the Sherpas, and other local groups, that the West first encountered stories of the fabled and rarely seen *metoh-kangmi*. This is another name for the Yeti. *Metoh* translates to "man-bear" and *kangmi* to "snowman." The origin of the term gets a little confused in 1921, when, during Charles Howard-Bury's expedition to Mount Everest, many footprints were discovered in the high altitudes. According to Howard-Bury, the Sherpa guides called them the tracks of a "metch-kangmi" or "filthy snowman." At the time, Henry Newman, a reporter for *The Statesman* in Kolkata, mistranslated the term as "abominable snowman." Consequently, the name Abominable Snowman began to be used for the Yeti in 1921. Newman's mistranslation was brought to light by English mountaineer Bill Tilman in his book, *Mount Everest 1938.*

ACCESS

For generations, the Himalayas were not easily accessible to outsiders. In part, this was because of the physical isolation. The British did gain access during the nineteenth century due to their colonization of India, but the trickle of British explorers never grew to a flood.

Politics has been another problem. The borders of Nepal were closed in 1816 after the country lost a war with India, and they were not opened again officially until 1951. The British occupied Tibet in 1904 and maintained control until a treaty was signed the following year. China invaded Tibet in 1950, and since then has occupied the small nation. From the beginning of the twentieth century until the end of World War II in 1945, it was almost impossible for any Westerner to enter the central Himalaya area legally. In fact, it wasn't until the 1950s that anyone was allowed back into the Himalayas, much less any scientific expeditions. And even then, the government could and did often require specific permissions that were very difficult to get. Yet with all these difficulties, some determined explorers did

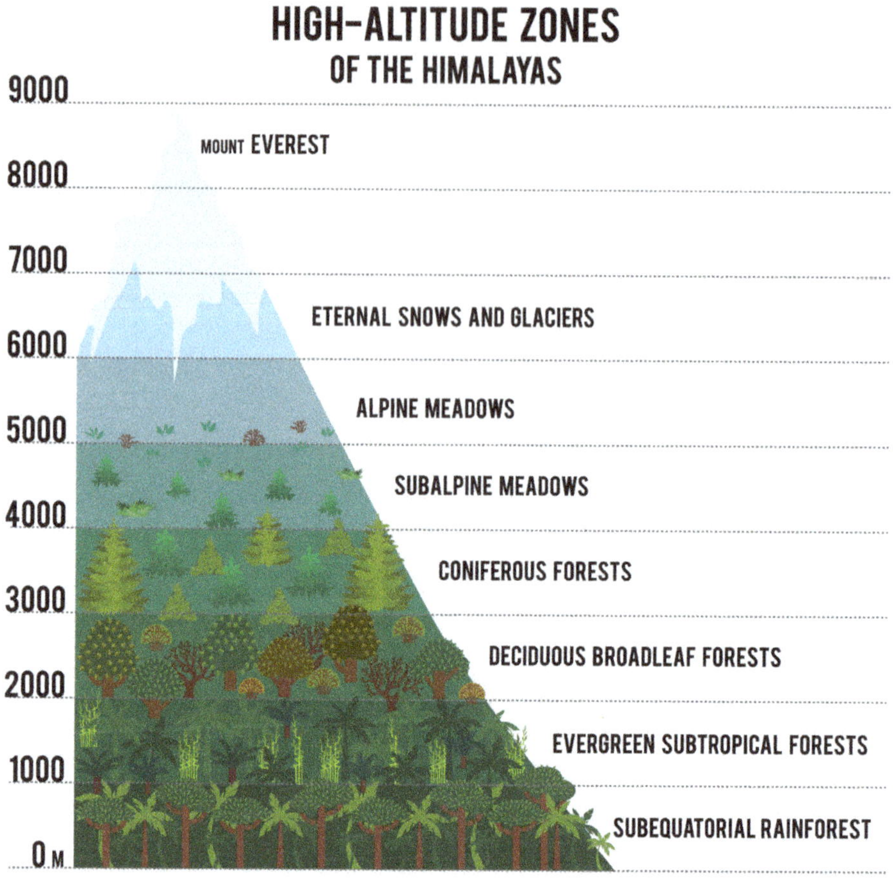

From the valleys and base of the Himalayas to the peaks, there is an incredible amount of biodiversity in the area. The region is home to ten thousand types of plants, as well as hundreds of different animal species.

make their way into the mountains, even prior to 1950. But once they were actually on-site, why were they not able to gather more specific proof of the Yeti's existence?

First, remember the landscape. Ranging from 22,000 (6,706 meters) to 29,000 feet (8,839 m) above sea level, the Himalayas are inhospitable to those not accus-

A TIMELINE OF EARLY ENCOUNTERS

1889 Major L. A. Waddell, while exploring the area of northeast Sikkim in the Himalayas, reports finding large, bearlike footprints in the snow well above the elevation at which any bear should be living. His Sherpa guides tell him it is a Yeti, a dangerous beast.

1913 A strange, very strong creature with a black monkey-like face and body covered in long silvery yellow fur is reportedly captured by Chinese hunters. The creature has hands and feet like a man. It dies after five months in captivity.

1921 Members of an expedition led by Lieutenant Colonel Charles Howard-Bury spot figures ahead of them while climbing Mount Everest. They find huge footprints of someone—or something—walking barefoot in the snowfield.

1923 On an Everest expedition, Major Alan Cameron reports seeing a line of figures moving along a cliff above the snowline. Two days later, photos are taken of footprints.

1936 Footprints are found in the outer reaches of the snowline by members of the H. W. Tilman expedition while nearing Mount Everest.

(continued on the next page)

(continued from the previous page)

1948 A Norwegian prospector, Jan Frostis, claims to have been attacked by one of two Yetis, in one of the rare physical encounters, while near Zemu Gap, in Sikkim. His shoulder is badly mangled.

1950 Mummified fingers and some skin are found in the Himalayas. Experts determine that the body parts are "almost human" but cannot identify the species.

1951 Explorer Eric Shipton takes photographs of huge footprints in the snow while climbing Mount Everest.

tomed to high altitudes, making travel a slow, careful business. Winters are harsh, and spring brings with it the heavy rains known as monsoons, which can create flash floods and mudslides. One bad storm could wipe out half an expedition if the party isn't ready for it. Second, there's the technology. Prior to 1950, cameras were large, bulky, expensive machines that were difficult to work properly in extreme temperatures, assuming the delicate pieces made it safely up the mountainside. Unlike today's point-and-shoot digital models and cell phone cameras, those earlier models needed training to handle and proper conditions in order to get the best results. At the upper levels of Mount Everest, the air temperature can get dangerously cold, down to -4°Fahrenheit (-20°Celsius). And the higher up one travels, the colder and more bitterly dry the air becomes. It's not healthy for people and most certainly it was no good for photographic film. Because of these technological limitations, most of the historical evidence comes from written journals and sketches, with only the occasional black-and-white photograph of a footprint.

This Tibetan man holds an alleged Yeti scalp at Pangboche Monastery in 1960. The scalp, as well as a supposed Yeti hand, were housed in the monastery for many years.

ARTIFACTS AND FOLKLORE

Even physical evidence is not clear-cut. Many Buddhist lamaseries—homes to religious figures called lamas, much as monasteries house monks—claimed to have relics, or religious objects, that came from the Yetis. Shamanistic relics of these sorts were used to remind Buddhists of their connection to the world around them, both in physical and spiritual terms. And, as such, stories would grow around these objects, both true and invented, to enhance their religious significance.

This is where the tradition of folklore comes from: the stretching of what might be or might have been into genuine storytelling. It is the job of the researcher to discover what among those stories is a verified encounter and what is myth, legend, or outright falsehood. David Gordon, author of *Field Guide to the Sasquatch,* wrote, "The absence of evidence is not necessarily evidence of an absence." In other words, lack of proof is no proof at all. The burden rests on both sides—believer and skeptic alike—to establish their cases.

For example, some skeptics insist that the so-called Yeti footprints that have been discovered in the snow of the Himalayas over the years are actually animal tracks that were misshapened as the snow melted. As prints melt, they become larger. Other doubters believe that the prints are those of holy men who at times go barefoot. As for other artifacts, some monks recount that the Yeti scalps are ancient religious objects that were made as wigs and worn by dancers who played Yeti characters in rituals. Others contend the scalps are likely made of goatskin. In any case, the details of artifacts and folklore hold clues to the truth, so long as they can be examined objectively.

CHAPTER TWO

THE YETI AND OTHER CRYPTIDS

Anyone who claims to encounter an unusual creature, and then shares his or her story, contributes to the public idea of that creature. And during moments of quick or frightening events, a person's reality can be altered, whether intentionally or not, from the truth of the event. Then, in recounting the story over and over again, facts become distorted: people and objects become larger and scarier, and actions become more outlandish, vivid, and deadly. Listeners become used to the story and add their own embellishments as they spread the tale, too.

The more witnesses there are to a cryptid encounter, the more effectively they can corroborate, or confirm, what they saw. Witnesses should record as many details as possible before discussing the story.

After time and many more tellings, each of the people, objects, and actions in the event seems to become even more dramatic. As a result, a legend is made out of an event that was not so dramatic to begin with. There is no way to determine what the truth of such a story is or to distinguish between embellished details and outright creation. The Yeti legend is much the same.

LOCAL MYTHOLOGY

How long has the Yeti been known to the people of the Himalayas? It is almost impossible to tell when the first report of the man-beast was made. Certainly, long before any Western observer came to Tibet or Nepal, the Yeti was already an established part of the local culture. Whether called Yeh-ti (Tibet), Nyalmo (on the Tibetan side of the Himalayas), Alma (in Russia), Teh-lma (in Nepal), or Kra-dhan (in Nepal), and no matter how the descriptions differed—the color of the hair or how much of the creature's body it covered—all the stories agreed: the creature walked upright, had huge feet, was the size of a man but much broader, and had hair covering most of its body. And it shied away from human interaction. The occasional traveler or hunter might encounter huge footprints in the snow or lose a goat under suspicious circumstances, but actual encounters were few and far between. There were, of course, claims that a Yeti—or packs of them—had damaged villages or towns but

AN UNUSUAL FIELD OF STUDY

Cryptozoology is the study of and search for animals, especially those that are from legends and myths, such as the Yeti and Bigfoot, to evaluate the likelihood of their existence. The word "cryptozoology" originated with Dr. Bernard Heuvelmans (1916–2001), a zoologist, jazz musician, comedian, and writer. The word comes from the Greek word *kryptos*, which means "hidden" or "mysterious," and zoology, the study of animals. The word then

Bernard Heuvelmans wrote about many so-called hidden animals, including sea serpents and the giant squid.

(continued on the next page)

(continued from the previous page)

refers to the study of hidden animals. Heuvelmans researched and studied various animals, trying to scientifically substantiate or debunk various rumors and legends over the years. In 1999, he donated his extensive documentation and specimens to the Museum of Zoology in Lausanne, Switzerland.

As Loren Coleman, another famous cryptozoologist, wrote in Heuvelmans's obituary in 2001, Huevelmans was dedicated to documenting evidence of cryptids in a scientific way, but because his subjects were so fantastical, he had to conduct his work without the support of any government or other organizational funding. Despite Huevelmans's experience as a zoologist and efforts to debunk certain rumors scientifically, however, his work has been criticized for seemingly sloppy research and a lack of analysis.

typically to look for food, not to intentionally cause damage to the settlements.

And yet if a traveler asked a local, they would be the first to assert that these were no mere beasts. Yetis serve a purpose, they would say, more than any wild animal roaming for food and shelter. In fact, according to one Sherpa legend, the Yetis were mysterious creatures that guarded the Himalayan slopes, standing between humanity and the unattainable peaks of the mountains that were inhabited by demon-spirits. As such, people were to be wary of them, but not actively afraid.

To discover the truth, modern expeditions, it might be assumed, would take with them modern equipment, allowing a much more accurate means to capture what proof they might find. This, however, is rarely the case. Although the technology has advanced, the cost for such tools has also increased. And though the explorers of the past, and the scientists of the early twentieth century, often had government backing to fund their supplies, modern Yeti researchers all too often work on a nonprofit basis, either on their own or through an organization that does not have the funds to equip them properly.

OTHER APELIKE CREATURES

Although the Yeti is one of the best-known ape-man creatures, there have been similar phenomena all over the world, most of which take place in areas much less remote than the Himalayas.

In the United States, Americans have the aptly named Bigfoot, or Sasquatch. This cryptid is to be found—at least according to the stories—in many states, from Florida up to the Canadian border, but the best-known stomping grounds are the woods of the Pacific Northwest region, where its legend first grew.

Big feet aside, the "ape man" is a familiar figure in folklore—both traditional and modern—all around the world, too. The figure goes as far back as ancient Sumeria and the story of Gilgamesh, whose companion Enkidu was a "wild man" who had to be taught human speech. In modern day, these cryptids are found between the pages of the *National Enquirer* and in the "Weird News" sections of other publications.

Sightings continue to occur everywhere. In Malaysia, eighteen-inch (46 cm) footprints made by a creature with a twelve-foot (3.7 m) stride were recorded in August 1966, feeding rumors of a huge apelike cryptid living deep within the jungle. Villagers claimed the beast was a shy, harmless giant. In the Philippines, a "massive hairy creature" known as the Kapre was reported to be noxious smelling but unthreatening, and it reportedly maintained a rudimentary kind of trade agreement with local villagers. In the former Soviet

The Yeti is generally described as apelike, bipedal, and covered with hair. Unlike the towering Sasquatch of North American forests, the Yeti is generally thought to be around 5 to 6 feet (1.5–1.8 m) tall.

Union, a creature called Snezhni Chelovyek inspired the formation of a government research program to investigate sightings during the 1950s, but the program was later abandoned.

In central Asia, close to the Yeti's home, the Alma is one local variant, which may simply be another name for the far-ranging Yeti. Another such variant is the Mande Burung, also known as the "forest man," in India. It's described as an exceedingly tall bipedal creature, standing at 10 feet (3 m), and is covered in black and gray fur. The Ban Manush, said to measure around 6 feet (1.8 m) tall, has been rumored to roam India, Nepal, and Bangladesh, too. And in Africa, long held to be the birthplace of all humanity, there is the Waterbobbejan, or "water baboon," of South Africa, and the Agogue, a more mischievous cousin, which has been spotted in Tanzania and along the Ivory Coast.

DECRYPTING CRYPTIDS

One thing to bear in mind when it comes to cryptids is that so many creatures were thought to be nothing but stories until actual animals with similar qualities were discovered. The Virunga Mountains, which are a range of extinct volcanoes bordering the Democratic Republic of Congo, Rwanda, and Uganda, are home to the mountain gorilla, a subspecies of gorilla that was a mystery for decades.

In 1847, missionary and naturalist Thomas Savage discovered the skull of a mountain gorilla and recognized it as a new species, but it wasn't until 1902 that the species was identified and given a name. What speculation must have occurred in the decades between discovery of the skull and identification of the species?

Mountain gorillas live in forests at high elevation, from 8,000 (2,438 m) to 13,000 feet (3,962 m), and have thick fur to help them survive when temperatures drop below freezing. As of 2018, they are considered a critically endangered species, but conservation efforts have helped increase their populations in the Virunga Mountains. Could the Yeti and its relatives be similar unknown primates of a dwindling population? More evidence is needed in order to find out.

CHAPTER THREE

THE SEARCH FOR EVIDENCE

The second half of the twentieth century brought with it explorers who were more organized and better prepared for the harsh environment of the Himalayan mountains than those who came before them. After the Nepalese and Tibetan governments opened their borders to outsiders once again, the late 1950s saw some incredible efforts to document the Yeti.

FOOTPRINTS IN THE SNOW

Eric Shipton was an experienced explorer, with half a dozen attempts to climb Mount Everest under his belt. In the winter of 1951, he and two companions were working their way across a neighboring mountain. They spotted a figure moving in the distance ahead of them, 20,000 feet (6,000 m) up on the slopes of the Menlung Glacier. They tracked the Yeti from there, but lost sight of it in an ice field. Shipton took a photograph of the creature's footprints. Those photos clearly showed the imprint of a foot that could have been that of a Yeti, an

Many regard the Shipton photo as strong evidence for the Yeti's existence, but others are not so sure. Skeptics note the irregular depressions within the footprint and the lack of other well-developed prints nearby.

unknown animal, or perhaps a bear. Photographed with an ice axe next to it, the clearest footprint measured between 12 and 13 inches (30.5 and 33 cm) long by about 7 inches (18.7 cm) wide. These footprints were not made by a human. The Shipton photograph is often held up as one of the best pieces of evidence of something living in the heights of the Himalayas.

ACTIVE SEARCHES FOR THE YETI

The 1950s saw a surge in quests for proof of the Yeti. Between 1951 and 1953, René de Nebesky-Wojkowitz, a Czech ethnologist and Tibetologist, fielded several Yeti explorations to Tibet. Unfortunately, the members of the excursions found nothing but some tracks that didn't look like they had come from any known animal living in the area. Not to be deterred, Nebesky-Wojkowitz suggested that this failure was due to the Yeti's superior mobility over rough terrain and an increased lung capacity that gave it an impressive advantage in those high, oxygen-starved elevations.

The *Daily Mail*, a British newspaper, funded a survey in 1954. Zoologists, naturalists, cameramen, and trained guides formed the expedition. They found tracks and droppings, which they claimed came from a Yeti, plus a scalp of coarse hair unlike human hair. The expedition was allowed to take one hair from

(continued on the next page)

(continued from the previous page)

that scalp out of the country, but no more. Test results on its origin were inconclusive.

In 1958, American scientist Dr. Norman Dyhrenfurth discovered caves in Kathmandu, Nepal, that showed evidence of having been inhabited by near-human creatures. He had plaster casts of footprints and hair samples as evidence. The results of testing on these samples at that time were inconclusive.

TOO SLICK

In 1956, Thomas Slick, a Texas oilman and millionaire with a longtime interest in trying to discover the truth behind the Yeti legend, gained the backing of the San Antonio Zoo. Such sponsorship allowed Slick's party to enter the Himalayas in 1957 as a legitimate, government-approved expedition. Thanks to Slick's money, the expedition came equipped with up-to-date scientific equipment, weapons, hounds to track the Yeti's scent, and enough men to cover a large area and question locals. Those interviews led Slick to speculate that there were actually two or three different types of Yetis, each living in a different area of Tibet.

He and his crews made several trips into the mountains between 1957 and 1959, coming back with photos, footprint castings, and—in a rather brazen act of smuggling that involved the aid of American actor James Stewart and his wife—two fingers from a mummified hand that locals claimed was that of a Yeti. Called the Pangboche hand for the location it was taken from, Slick's team replaced the stolen fingers with human ones so their theft would not be quickly noticed, then slipped the mummified digits into the luggage of the Stewarts, trusting that the luggage of such world-famous people would not be searched.

The Stewarts arrived safely in London, but their luggage didn't! It was lost between flights, and the scientists had to assume that even if the luggage was found, their prized piece of evidence would be

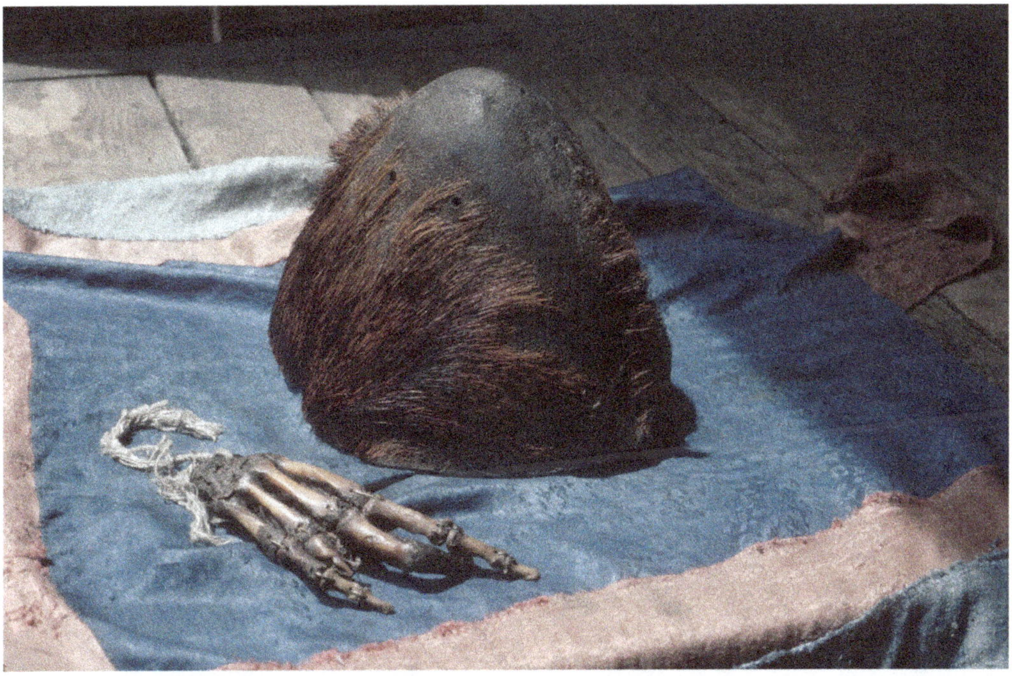

The Pangboche hand and scalp were thought to have come from a Yeti that a monk once saw in a cave. After twentieth-century attempts to examine these artifacts, the truth has only become more elusive.

discovered and confiscated. However, the luggage was returned to the Stewarts soon after, still unsearched.

So what happened to all this evidence? No one is quite sure. Loren Coleman, in his book *Tom Slick and the Search for the Yeti,* mentions that a footprint cast and hair were reportedly sent to *Life* magazine, which had been "consulting" with Slick on his discoveries. It may be that they are still stored somewhere in a warehouse, unmarked and forgotten.

ATTEMPTS TO REFUTE THE YETI

The Slick expeditions should have been enough to make the search for the Yeti a reputable scientific venture. But Sir Edmund Hillary, renowned as the first Westerner to climb Mount Everest, was determined to debunk the Yeti myth once and for all.

In 1960, a scientific expedition sponsored by World Book, Inc., went into the Himalayas, led by Sir Edmund Hillary and Marlin Perkins, who would in later years star in the nature documentary series *Wild Kingdom.* During their three months in the field, they investigated the "proof" Slick's team claimed to have found. And it was here that the Pangboche hand came back to haunt Tom Slick. With the human fingers added, its veracity—along with that of other pelts and scalps—was thrown into serious doubt. The World Book expedition's report that the Yeti was nothing more than a myth was more newsworthy than Slick's claims to the contrary, and they had the weight

Sir Edmund Hillary (*left*), Colonel John Hunt (*center*), and Sherpa guide Tenzing Norgay (*right*) examine a model showing the route Hillary and Tenzing took as the first men to reach the top of Mount Everest in 1953.

of public opinion on their side, including articles in *Life* and *National Geographic,* among others, and a traveling road show in the mid 1960s featuring Perkins and Hillary.

BIOLOGY AND "WILD MEN"

Some researchers claim that the Yeti and its kin around the world are "wild men," perhaps direct descendants of the first primates to come out of

Africa, and evolved into having intelligence that was near to that of humans. Others think the Yeti is a modern but not yet identified ape, a closer relative to the gorilla than to humans. But one of the most plausible scenarios offered to date involves *Gigantopithecus,* which was the largest primate to live on Earth. It stood almost ten feet (3 m) high and weighed close to 600 pounds (272 kilograms). This great ape lived during the Pleistocene era, 1.8 million to 10,000 years ago. The fossil record from that time shows that it lived in the area that is now China and Southeast Asia.

According to scientists, *Gigantopithecus* looked very much like today's gorilla, not walking upright on two feet but using arms and knuckles to cover ground more efficiently on four limbs. Fossil records also suggest that its dietary habits were much the same as its modern descendants—mostly vegetarian. If so, scientists can assume that its behavior might also mimic that of modern gorillas: shy and retiring creatures that nonetheless can become quite aggressive when they are threatened. Some animals that have survived from the time of the *Gigantopithecus* include the orangutan and tapir of southeastern Asia, as well as the giant panda of southwestern China.

There are enough similarities in appearance and overlap in territory that the link between the Yeti and *Gigantopithecus* cannot be dismissed out of hand. Is it possible that a branch of this ancient family did not die out some 500,000 years ago, as always thought? Because there is no obvious reason why *Gigantopithe-*

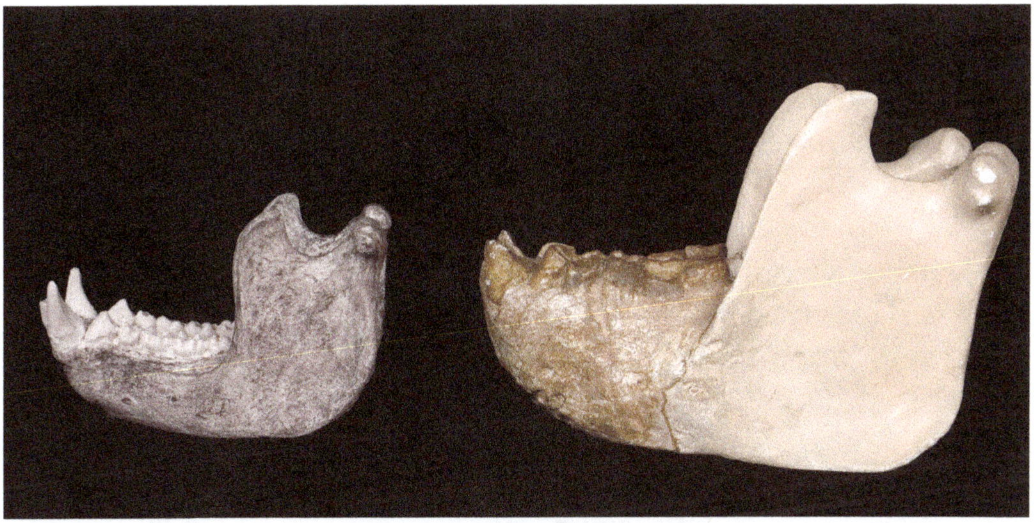

The *Gigantopithecus* jaw (*right*), as compared to the gorilla jaw (*left*), gives scientists an idea of how large *Gigantopithecus* was. The central part of the jaw is a fossil fragment, while the rest is a reconstruction.

cus became extinct, save for a probable failure to adapt to changes in the climate during the Ice Age, it is possible that such a branch does exist. Certainly the remoteness of the region would aid such a race in remaining undiscovered until only recently. This would explain the scant reports of such creatures until the nineteenth century.

The arguments against this theory are that *Gigantopithecus* theoretically stood between 8 (2.4 m) and 10 feet (3 m) tall, while the Yeti reportedly average 5 feet (1.5 m) tall—barely the size of an adult human. It is possible that the species might have shrunk, but such a great difference between those average heights makes this seem unlikely.

Other researchers claim that the Yeti might be a descendant of humans' own ancestor, the Neanderthal. The height would certainly be a better match, but the reported hairiness of the Yeti gives pause: Neanderthals would have been no hairier than the average *Homo sapiens*, or modern humans. Both these theories take a heavy blow when faced with the fact that the last Neanderthal has been dated at 40,000 BCE, and *Gigantopithecus* was last seen in the fossil record at 500,000 BCE. Without more recent fossil records, it is almost impossible to draw a connection that will stand up to scientific scrutiny.

CHAPTER FOUR

CONTEMPORARY FINDINGS

There have been so many challenges in the search for evidence of the Yeti, from the possibility that sightings may be due to hallucinations caused by high altitude and the resulting lack of oxygen, to charlatans looking to profit from a hoax. Such factors can muddy the waters for those who are looking for the truth, but footprints, perplexing droppings and hairs, and the long history of consistent reporting by many people offer hope for a positive answer. Although the *Gigantopithecus* fossil record may not have an answer, other such records still might.

DR. MEAVE LEAKEY

In 1999, a group of paleontologists led by Dr. Meave Leakey found a skull and partial jawbone in northern Kenya. After careful study, it was determined that the nearly complete skull was 3.5 million years old and belonged to a completely different genus and species than they had expected. Leakey named the new genus *Kenyanthropus platyops* (meaning, flat-faced man of

Kenya). However, some scientists classify the fossil as a separate species of *Australopithecus*. Whereas before, scientists thought that modern *Homo sapiens* had descended from Lucy (*Australopithecus afarensis*), the fossil species that dated back 3.5 to 4 million years, it may be that humans' family tree has a great many branches—and the founding parent of humans' own specific branch is in doubt. If this is the case, then who is to say that the Yeti cannot exist—and in fact, may be a cousin of humans, descended from a three-million-year-old branch?

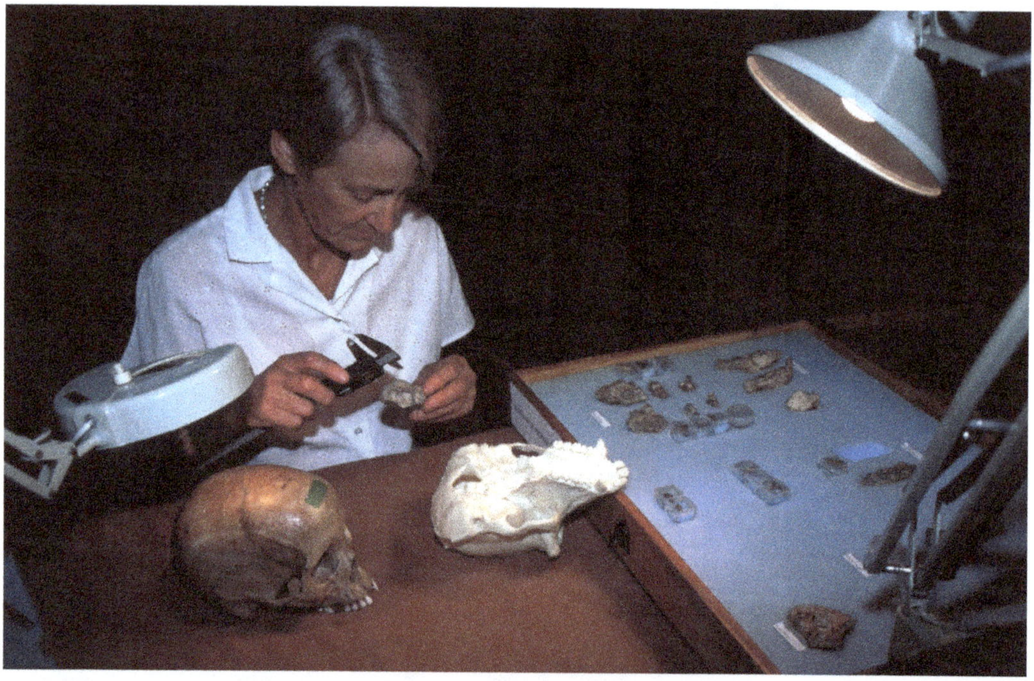

Meave Leakey has done a lot of work in the Lake Turkana region of Kenya. She and other scientists in the area use modern geographic tools, such as GPS coordinates, to keep track of areas that have been explored.

According to Leakey, when hominids split off from the great apes and began walking upright, it would make sense that they would wander into different territories and adapt to their new homes. If one of these offshoot branches were to have wandered from Africa into the highlands of Asia, it would certainly have developed a coat of hair to protect itself from the cold; larger feet, like a snowshoe rabbit, to run along the surface of the snow; and many other characteristics that could describe the Yeti.

Just when people think science has given them an answer, more discoveries cast new light on old evidence.

THE FLORES MAN

In 2004, Henry Gee, the senior editor of *Nature,* an international weekly science journal, wrote an article entitled "Flores, God and Cryptozoology." In the article, he implied that the discovery of some fossils called *Homo floresiensis* ("Flores Man" and nicknamed the Hobbit) on the island of Flores in Indonesia in 2003 could raise the hopes of Yeti hunters. *Homo floresiensis,* a potential dwarf-size relative of humans, is now extinct. According to Gee, "The discovery that *Homo floresiensis* survived until so very recently, in geological terms, makes it more likely that stories of other mythical, human-like creatures such as yetis are founded on grains of truth."

However, scientists have continued to study *Homo floresiensis* since its discovery, and updates to its place in

TEAM EFFORT FROM JAPAN

In October 2008, members of a Japanese expedition to the Himalayan region of Nepal and Tibet photographed footprints that they believed might have been made by a Yeti. The group was called Yeti Project Japan, and its leader, Yoshiteru Takahashi, professed to have seen a Yeti on a journey he made five years earlier. He described the creature as being half-man and half-ape, walking on two legs like a human, and standing about 5 feet (1.5 m) tall.

According to the *Guardian* newspaper in the United Kingdom, the prints found by the group measured about 8 inches (20 cm) long and were human-like in appearance. The Japanese explorers discovered the prints at an altitude of about 15,748 feet (4,800 m) on Dhaulagiri IV, a mountain in the subrange of the Himalayas in western Nepal. According to a team member, "We saw three footprints which looked like that of human beings." The team spent more than forty days on Dhaulagiri IV, which is about 25,135 feet (7,661 m) high. The explorers said that they had seen traces of the Yeti in the past, although they could not provide any photographic evidence of the creature itself. They did take photos of the footprints though, and have asserted they are able to distinguish between the tracks of various other animals

on the mountainside. Team members maintained the footprints were unique, and announced their intention to keep up the search: Takahashi said the team would continue to hunt for the Yeti until they capture the creature on film. However, no updates on their efforts have become available since then.

history have been made. The skeletal remains were originally believed to have come from between ninety-five and twelve thousand years ago, but as an update in a 2016 issue of *Nature* revealed, new evidence suggested the remains were actually dated to between around one hundred thousand and sixty thousand years ago. It's unclear what this might mean in relation to the possibility of the Yeti, but updating the fossil record can help scientists determine exactly where such a creature might fit.

THE ECOLOGY QUESTION

American scholar Daniel C. Taylor, who has worked for decades on social change and community-led conservation, has formed an interesting theory about what the Yeti might really be. His 2017 book, *Yeti: The Ecology of a Mystery*, details his own expeditions in the Barun Valley of the Himalayas, as well as evidence he has found to support the idea that footprints like the ones Eric Shipton photographed were actually made by an Asiatic black bear.

Asiatic black bears are omnivores, like many other bears, and they have a varied diet that includes fruits, seeds, and nuts. They spend much of their time foraging high in the trees and are skilled climbers.

The biggest mystery of the Shipton photo has been the apparent thumb in the print. Taylor found similar footprints in the lush Barun Valley, and a local hunter he worked with said he thought they were from a tree bear (most likely an Asiatic black bear). As Taylor told *National Geographic* in August 2017:

> Suddenly we had an explanation for where the thumb came from. A bear that lives in a tree forces an inner digit down so it can make an opposable grip. Normal bears cannot make an opposable grip. But if you're spending a lot of time in the tree, you train that one thumb to grab a branch or break bamboo.

THE BARUN VALLEY

Makalu-Barun National Park is the only protected area with an elevation gain of 26,000 feet (8,000 m). The area includes tropical forests as well as snowy peaks.

Daniel Taylor's work in the Barun Valley has included years of collaboration with the local community to protect the area and the bears native to it. As Taylor explained to *National Geographic*, "In [my] search for the Yeti, I had stumbled into, arguably, the greatest wilderness

DEBUNK IT!

As DNA analysis became a more viable option for scientists interested in the Yeti, it seemed like an answer might be in reach. In 2014, an Oxford University genetics professor named Dr. Bryan Sykes called for any suspected Yeti samples to be sent to him for DNA analysis. Hair, fingernails, and bone fragments were all tested, but most of the samples originated from bears or sheep. Sykes did find, however, that he could not fully identify the DNA sequences in two samples, and he published his research with mention of these alluring anomalies. Interest in the Yeti spiked yet again, and the following became clear:

- Sykes and his colleagues asserted the DNA was from unknown species, even though they knew not all known species of bear in the region had their DNA documented.
- Their analysis was based on very short, incomplete sequences of DNA.
- Doctoral students checked Sykes's sequences and found he had made a mistake—they were simply incomplete sequences, and had come from known species.
- Sykes and his colleagues did not question a hunter who provided one sample—he had said he was very familiar with brown bears, yet he

was confused by the behavior of the bearlike creature from whic he had claimed the sample.

The study highlighted how the excitement of a sensational topic can affect people's work. Sykes's analysis was aimed toward proving the Yeti must exist, when the truth is a scientist must be unbiased and present his or her results objectively in order to contribute valuable work in his or her field.

on the planet. But it was not a protected area ... I decided to take my family heritage of community-based solutions in healthcare and apply it to nature protection, working with the local community to manage the whole landscape rather than just creating pockets." The area is home to Makalu-Barun National Park, and Taylor worked with the community to create a "Yeti Trail," allowing tourists to walk through a pristine, wild park in the highest place on Earth. Even if scientists one day determine that the Yeti is in fact a myth, increased tourism and conservation efforts in the Barun Valley area are positive consequences of people's interest in the creature.

CHAPTER FIVE

LIFE OF THE YETI IN POP CULTURE

The Yeti has become a surprisingly well-used icon, from advertisements and amusement parks to literature and movies. The Yeti name has even been used for different camping equipment products, invoking the wild and cold of the outdoors. Every year in George, Washington, the Sasquatch! Music Festival is held in the Gorge Amphitheatre, and one of the stages is the Yeti Stage. This shy cryptid of the Himalayan mountains has certainly reached the public consciousness, and this helps keep interest in finding it alive.

PERSISTENCE IN THE HILLS

Joshua Gates and his team, who work on the television series *Destination Truth*, reported discovering footprints in Nepal, in the area near Mount Everest, in December 2007. The team made plaster casts of the footprints, and a scientist at Idaho State University studied them. Gates said that the scientist did not believe the prints were made by humans or by a bear. He did think, though, that they were human-like. In 2009, Gates's team found hair from a creature in Bhutan. A forensics laboratory in

Texas examined the hair samples and concluded that they were from a primate, one that has not yet been identified by scientists.

British scientists found hairs in the Garo Hills area of northeast India in July 2008 and had them analyzed by the Oxford Brookes University in England. Originally, the tests were inconclusive. The samples were found to be similar to those collected by Hillary's expedition group in the 1950s. Lab analyses have since revealed that the hair came from the Himalayan goral, also called a gray goral. This mammal looks like a brownish gray or reddish goat and has backward-curving and pointed horns.

Himalayan gorals are crepuscular, meaning they are most active during early morning and evening hours. They relax in caves or on cliffs during the day, and the color of their fur camouflages them against the rocks.

THE YETI BRANCHES OUT

As the search continues on television, in the "Weird News" sections of various publications, and in various labs, the Yeti's name and features have branched out. People now associate the Yeti with so much more than the Himalayan myth it comes from, and the examples are numerous. The Yeti has been used as a mascot for the Czech automobile manufacturer Skoda, which made the mini SUV Yeti beginning in 2009. Walt Disney World's Expedition Everest, an attraction at Disney's Animal Kingdom Asia theme park in Florida, has a high, fast

This Yeti ice sculpture was part of the grand opening of Disney World's Expedition Everest. The ride takes visitors careening through a Himalayan mountain setting, while swerving to avoid the Yeti's clutches.

roller coaster that includes the snarling Yeti creature at the mountain's summit. In addition to the roller coaster in this theme park, there is a Yak & Yeti Restaurant at the base of Mount Everest in the town of Anandapur. In California's Disneyland, there is a high-speed amusement ride called the Matterhorn Bobsleds that plunges riders into caves and hurls them into the air, bringing them near the dens of the audio-animatronic Abominable Snowmen who lurk and growl among the mountain's cliffs.

FROM THE SLOPES TO THE SCREEN

Over the years there have been several important films in which Yetis play a part as well. *The Snow Creature* (1954), directed by W. Lee Wilder, is about an American botanical expedition to the Himalayas where the members, including a news photographer and a local Sherpa guide whose wife is kidnapped by a Yeti, discover a Yeti den while they are searching for the guide's wife. They capture one of the creatures and take it back to Los Angeles, California, where it escapes during an argument with customs about whether the creature is an animal or a human. Meanwhile, the Yeti kills whoever gets in his way.

As far as the Yeti in animation goes, Warner Brothers Cartoons has produced some *Looney Tunes* episodes with Abominable Snowman or Yeti figures, particularly the 1961 "The Abominable Snow Rabbit," starring Bugs Bunny and Daffy Duck. The two cartoon characters plan

OF MYTHS AND MONSTERS

In 2010, the Horniman Museum in London, England, put on a temporary exhibition about mythical monsters, entitled "Myths and Monsters." The museum was one of several locations for the traveling exhibition originally organized by the Natural History Museum in London. (The scientists at the Natural History Museum were the experts who analyzed the "Yeti scalp," which Sir Edmund Hillary had borrowed for further study during his expeditions to the Himalayas in the 1960s.)

The display included animatronic models of the Cyclops, unicorn, Yeti, mermaid, dragon, and chimera, among other creatures. The museum took visitors on a journey to discover what was truth and what was fiction regarding the ancient myths and legends, and it presented a variety of scientific evidence that offered explanations about the myths' origins and merits. The exhibit investigated the links between dinosaurs and dragons and whether the Yeti could be an actual living creature.

to dig their way underground to sunny Palm Springs, California, but take a wrong turn and end up in the snow-covered Himalayas. They run into the Abominable Snowman, who gives them some trouble and follows them to Palm Springs, where he finally melts away in the overwhelming heat.

In the animated feature *Monsters, Inc.*, the Yeti is a kind-hearted monster who makes snow cones and wishes people would think of him as the "Adorable Snowman" instead of an "Abominable" one.

In 1964, the stop-motion animation Christmas special, *Rudolph the Red-Nosed Reindeer*, aired on the NBC television network. Rudolph and his friend Hermey the Elf encounter the Abominable Snow Monster of the North while in the woods. The monster dislikes Christmas but loves to eat reindeer, and so he chases them. Eventually, the Abominable Snow Monster captures Rudolph and his family in his cave. Friends come to the rescue by clobbering the monster and pulling out his teeth. Near the end of the movie, the Abominable Snow Monster has second thoughts, and he puts a star on the top of the Christmas tree and is welcomed in Christmastown.

In 2001, the animated *Monsters, Inc.*, produced by the Pixar Animation Studios and released by Walt Disney Pictures, is about monsters who are professional scarers. The monsters sneak into children's bedrooms to make them scream. They then convert the screams into energy to power Monstropolis, a city without humans, and to keep the town running. One of the monsters is the Abominable Snowman, the voice of which is supplied by actor

John Ratzenberger. A little human girl accidentally enters the city, and the good, kind-hearted monsters attempt to return her to her home before the bad, mean-spirited monsters try to thwart their efforts.

BETWEEN THE PAGES

The Yeti has famously made appearances in literature as well. R. L. Stine wrote a children's book entitled *The Abominable Snowman of Pasadena* in his Goosebumps series, which was published by Scholastic in 2003. The characters Jordan Blake and his sister, Nicole, are tired of the heat in Pasadena, California, and end up taking a trip to Alaska where they experience a real winter. Their father has been hired to photograph a mysterious huge snow creature known as the Abominable Snowman. The monster ends up chasing Jordan and Nicole.

In *The Adventures of Tintin*, a comic strip series, the Belgian artist George Rémi (1907–1983), who worked under the pen name Hergé, created a Yeti story called "Tintin in Tibet." The hero, a young reporter named Tintin, travels to Tibet to rescue a Chinese friend, Chang Chong-Chen, who is involved in a plane crash in the Himalayas. While in Tibet, the rescue team discovers footprints in the snow that resemble Yeti prints. After a series of mishaps, including being buried in an avalanche, the group finds Chang in a cave with the Yeti, who has befriended him. The team rescues Chang, who is convinced that the Yeti is not a wild beast but a being with a human soul.

In the Marvel Comics Universe, the Abominable Snowman is a character, originally appearing in *Tales to Astonish*, No. 13. The story revolves around Carl Hanson who is in Calcutta (Kolkata) and who overhears someone speaking about a photograph that he owns showing the Abominable Snowman. Hanson steals the photo and journeys to the Himalayas to find the monster. He doesn't get any help from the local people because they know that the photo is cursed and they recommend that Hanson get rid of it before it destroys him. Consequently, Hanson hunts for the monster himself, only to grow to resemble the Abominable Snowman as he

In 2006, the Dalai Lama presented the Light of Truth Award to the Hergé Foundation for *Tintin in Tibet*, as the book was a positive introduction to the Tibetan landscape and culture to many people worldwide.

climbs higher up into the mountains. Eventually, he loses his mind and drops the photo, which now mirrors what he has become.

In DC Comics, the fictional character Snowman, a villain, appears in *Batman*, No. 337. Snowman has a special gene that allows him to create and control snow and ice. He also has superhuman strength. Snowman, or Klaus Kristin, is the son of a male Yeti and a woman named Katrina Kristin. Snowman went to Gotham City to freeze it and runs up against Batman. In No. 522, Batman goes to Tibet to hunt the Snowman, and he ends up fighting him and Snowman's father, the Yeti. Snowman supposedly dies during the battle with Batman.

THE FUTURE OF THE YETI

There are many mysterious creatures throughout history and science that defy common sense. They fascinate people—and have for centuries—and may continue to elude those people who wish to definitely prove or disprove their existence. For skeptics, the Yeti or Abominable Snowman has never existed, and what evidence has appeared has been the result of human hoaxes. For believers, footprint tracks in the snow, photographs, and new sightings are enough to prove that ape-men creatures truly exist.

Whether the Yeti is a bear, a primate, or an unknown hominoid of some kind, the legend surrounding the creature persists. The important thing is to appreciate the cultural significance of such stories and figures and to support valid scientific studies that teach humanity more about the world. Even if Daniel Taylor's theory of the Yeti as a bear is right, the world has not lost a mythical creature because of his efforts—it has gained protection for one of the most beautiful places in the world and allowed access to it in a way that serves the area and its community. So many scientific discoveries occur because of mistakes, or because the person was looking for one thing and something unexpected fell into his or her lap—maybe the Yeti as it has been imagined will be discovered in a similar way one day. Until then, the Yeti's place as a popular myth remains securely in place.

GLOSSARY

Abominable Snowman Also known as Yeti, a legendary hairy, humanoid creature that is said to live in the Himalayas.

animatronic Lifelike robots or models that move electronically.

Bigfoot The North American version of the Yeti, frequently spotted along the U.S. and Canadian border, especially in Washington State.

botanical Of or relating to plants.

Buddhism An Asian religion and philosophy founded in northeastern India around 525 BCE by Siddhartha Gautama, who was called the Buddha.

carnivores Animals that feed on flesh.

crepuscular Referring to an animal that is most active in the early morning and evening.

cryptid A "hidden" animal, or animal whose existence has not been proven.

elusive Difficult to find, capture, or achieve.

ethnologist A scientist who studies the characteristics of various peoples and the differences and relationships between them.

genus A grouping of organisms having common characteristics distinct from those of other groupings.

glacier A mass of ice typically found in extremely cold climates such as Alaska, formed by snow that is compressed into granular ice. Glaciers move at a slow pace, pushed forward by gravity and their own weight.

Himalayas One of the greatest mountain ranges in the entire world, reaching from Pakistan through India, to Tibet and Nepal.

Hinduism A major religious and cultural tradition of India, which was developed from the Vedic religion.

hominid Humans and their primate ancestors.

monsoon A seasonal wind that brings heavy rains in parts of south and southeastern Asia.

Neanderthal An ancient subspecies of *Homo sapiens*.

Pleistocene era A time period in Earth's history, which began roughly 1.8 million years ago and ended 11,000 years ago, during which much of the world was covered by water or ice.

primate A mammal in an order that includes apes, monkeys, lemurs, and humans.

proverbial Referring to a particular proverb or idiom.

Sherpa A people living in Nepal who have a reputation for being the best mountain climbers and guides in the world.

Tibetologist A person who studies subjects relating to Tibet, including its history, religion, language, and culture.

Yeti The common name given to the two-legged, hairy creature frequently spotted in the Himalayas in Tibet and Nepal; also known as the Abominable Snow-man.

Alberta Sasquatch Organization
Website: http://sasquatchalberta.com
Facebook: @albertasasquatchorganization
YouTube: @MountainBeastMysteries
The Alberta Sasquatch Organization is a team of dedicated researchers and investigators who have created a public database of Sasquatch sightings in the Alberta, Canada.

The Bigfoot Field Researchers Organization (BFRO)
(408) 634-2376
Website: http://www.bfro.net
Twitter: @BFRO_Updates
Founded in 1995, BFRO explores the mystery of Bigfoot and maintains a database of sightings.

British Columbia Scientific Cryptozoology Club (BCSCC)
8805 Hudson Street, Suite 2305
Vancouver, BC V6P 4M9
Canada
Website: http://bcscc.ca/blog
Founded by journalists and scientists, BCSCC is Canada's leading cryptozoology organization. They engage in fieldwork all over the world year-round and are dedicated to following the accepted procedures of traditional zoology in their studies.

International Cryptozoology Museum
661 Congress Street
Portland, ME 04104

(207) 518-9496
Website: http://www.cryptozoologymuseum.com
Facebook: @cryptozoologymuseum
Billed as the world's only fully public cryptozoology museum, the exhibits include an 8-foot (2.4 m) tall, 400-pound (181 kg) Bigfoot; a mermaid; a thunderbird; and other "mysteries of the world."

Natural History Museum
Cromwell Road
London SW7 5BD
United Kingdom
+44 (0)20 7942 5000
Website: http://nhm.ac.uk
Facebook: @naturalhistorymuseum
Twitter: @NHM_London
The Natural History Museum sponsored a traveling exhibition called *Myths and Monsters* and includes displays and specimens about the Yeti and Abominable Snowman.

North American Wood Ape Conservancy
PO Box 2162
Belton, TX 76513
Website: http://www.woodape.org
Facebook: @noamwoodape
The North American Wood Ape Conservancy is a nonprofit scientific-research organization comprised of investigators, scientists, and naturalists who pursue education and research relating to the centuries-old "wildman" or "hairy man" phenomenon in North America.

Sasquatch Information Society
PO Box 48333
Seattle, WA 98148
Website: http://www.bigfootinfo.org
Facebook: @bigfootinfo
This organization provides a database containing Bigfoot news, articles, links, polls, events, sightings, interviews, and research.

FOR FURTHER READING

Chapman, Simon. *Himalayas: Bottom to Top*. London, UK: Collins, 2017.

Hoena, Blake. *Surviving Mount Everest: An Interactive Extreme Sports Adventure*. North Mankato, MN: Capstone Press, 2018.

Hurn, Samantha. *Anthropology and Cryptozoology: Researching Encounters with Mysterious Creatures*. New York, NY: Routledge, 2017.

Loxton, Daniel, and Donald R. Prothero. *Abominable Science! Origins of the Yeti, Nessie, and Other Famous Cryptids*. New York, NY: Columbia University Press, 2015.

Niver, Heather Moore. *Investigating Bigfoot, the Loch Ness Monster, and Other Cryptids*. New York, NY: Britannica Educational Publishing, 2017.

Niver, Heather Moore. *Sir Edmund Hillary Explores Mount Everest*. New York, NY: PowerKids Press, 2018.

Redfern, Nick. *The Monster Book: Creatures, Beasts, and Fiends of Nature*. Detroit, MI: Visible Ink Press, 2017.

Sexton, Martin. *The Yeti Society*. London, UK: Aeon Books Ltd, 2017.

Sykes, Bryan. *Bigfoot, Yeti, and the Last Neanderthal: A Geneticist's Search for Modern Apemen*. Newburyport, MA: Disinformation Books, 2016.

Tattersall, Ian, and Peter Névraumont. *Hoax: A History of Deception: 5,000 Years of Fakes, Forgeries, and Fallacies*. New York, NY: Black Dog & Leventhal Publishers, 2018.

Taylor, Daniel C. *Yeti: The Ecology of a Mystery*. New York, NY: Oxford University Press, 2017.

BIBLIOGRAPHY

Budd, Deena West. *The Weiser Guide to Cryptozoology: Werewolves, Dragons, Skyfish, Lizard Men, and Other Fascinating Creatures Real and Mysterios.* San Francisco, CA: Weiser Books, 2010.

Childress, David. *Yetis, Sasquatch & Hairy Giants.* Kempton, IL: Adventures Unlimited Press, 2010.

Christensen, Jen. "Science Solves the Mystery of the Elusive Yeti." CNN, November 29, 2017. https://www.cnn.com/2017/11/28/health/yeti-scientific-proof-study/index.html.

Coleman, Loren, and Patrick Huyghe. *Field Guide to Bigfoot, Yeti, and Other Mystery Primates Worldwide.* New York, NY: Harper Perennial, 1999.

Crompton, Samuel Willard. *Sir Edmund Hillary* (Great Explorers). New York, NY: Chelsea House Publishers, 2009.

Dennett, Preston. *Bigfoot, Yeti, and Other Ape-Men* (Mysteries, Legends, and Unexplained Phenomena). New York, NY: Chelsea House Publishers, 2010.

Eysenck, Juliet. "Does the Yeti Exist? Scientists Use DNA Evidence in Bid to Solve Mystery of the Abominable Snowman." *Telegraph*, May 30, 2016. https://www.telegraph.co.uk/science/2016/05/28/does-the-yeti-exist-scientists-use-dna-evidence-in-bid-to-solve.

Hall, Mark A., and Loren Coleman. *True Giants: Is Gigantopithecus Still Alive?* San Antonio, TX: Anomalist Books, 2010.

Hillary, Edmund. *High Adventure: The True Story of the First Ascent of Everest.* New York, NY: Oxford University Press, 2003.

McKenzie, Steven. "Scientists Challenge 'Abominable

Snowman DNA' Results." BBC News, December 17, 2014. http://www.bbc.com/news/uk-scotland-highlands-islands-30479718.

Naish, Darren. "Tales from the Cryptozoologicon: The Yeti." *Scientific American*, August 4, 2013. https://blogs.scientificamerican.com/tetrapod-zoology/tales-from-the-cryptozoologicon-the-yeti.

Noik, Sherry. "Meet Yeti, the So-called Abominable Snowman that Science Yet Again Says Is Just a Bear." *CBC News*, November 28, 2017. http://www.cbc.ca/news/technology/yeti-dna-tested-1.4417918.

Perkins, Sid. "So Much for the Abominable Snowman. Study Finds that 'Yeti' DNA Belongs to Bears." *Science*, November 28, 2017. http://www.sciencemag.org/news/2017/11/so-much-abominable-snowman-study-finds-yeti-dna-belongs-bears.

Sutikna, Thomas. "Revised Stratigraphy and Chronology for *Homo floresiensis* at Liang Bua in Indonesia." *Nature*, April 21, 2016. https://www.nature.com/articles/nature17179.

Worrall, Simon. "This Man Searched for the Yeti for 60 Years—and Found It." *National Geographic*, August 19, 2017. https://news.nationalgeographic.com/2017/08/yeti-abominable-snowman-bear-daniel-taylor.

ABOUT THE AUTHORS

Jenna Vale is a New Jersey native who has followed paranormal stories all her life. She has visited multiple sites of paranormal phenomena, from the dusty roads of *Weird NJ* fame to the haunted vaults of Edinburgh, Scotland.

Laura Anne Gilman, a writer and editor, lives in New York City.

PHOTO CREDITS

Cover © iStockphoto.com/yanishka; pp. 1, 7, 17, 25, 35, 44 (background) sakkmesterke/Shutterstock.com; p. 3 iprostocks /Shutterstock.com; pp. 4–5 (background) Mordolff/E+/Getty Images; p. 5 Alexander Yu. Zotov/Shutterstock.com; pp. 8–9 Antiqua Print Gallery/Alamy Stock Photo; p. 10 Education Images/Universal Images Group/Getty Images; p. 12 alinabel/Shutterstock.com; pp. 15, 31 Popperfoto/Getty Images; p. 17 Ed Vebell/Archive Photos /Getty Images; p. 19 Alain Benainous/Gamma-Rapho/Getty Images; p. 22 RikoBest/Shutterstock.com; p. 26 Topical Press Agency/Hulton Archive/Getty Images; p. 29 Ernst Haas/Getty Images; p. 33 Natural History Museum, London, UK/Bridgeman Images; p. 36 ullstein bild /Getty Images; p. 40 Gonzalo Azumendi/Stockbyte/Getty Images; p. 41 Grant Dixon/Lonely Planet Images/Getty Images; p. 45 jatesada natayo/Alamy Stock Photo; p. 46 Gustavo Caballero/Getty Images; p. 49 © Buena Vista Pictures/Courtesy Everett Collection; p. 51 John van Hasselt - Corbis/Corbis Historical/Getty Images; cover, back cover, and interior pages (caution pattern) Geschaft/Shutterstock.com.

Design: Michael Moy; Editor: Megan Kellerman; Photo Researcher: Karen Huang

Zoo Animals

GORILLAS AT THE ZOO

By Finn Ward

Gareth Stevens
PUBLISHING

Please visit our website, www.garethstevens.com. For a free color catalog of all our high-quality books, call toll free 1-800-542-2595 or fax 1-877-542-2596.

Library of Congress Cataloging-in-Publication Data

Ward, Finn.
Gorillas at the zoo / Finn Ward.
pages cm. — (Zoo animals)
Includes index.
ISBN 978-1-4824-2597-0 (pbk.)
ISBN 978-1-4824-2598-7 (6 pack)
ISBN 978-1-4824-2599-4 (library binding)
1. Gorilla—Juvenile literature. 2. Zoo animals—Juvenile literature. I. Title.
QL737.P94W37 2016
599.884—dc23
2015002596

First Edition

Published in 2016 by
Gareth Stevens Publishing
111 East 14th Street, Suite 349
New York, NY 10003

Editor: Ryan Nagelhout
Designer: Katelyn E. Reynolds

Photo credits: Cover, p. 1 Elena Blokhina/Shutterstock.com; p. 5 GTS Productions/Shutterstock.com; p. 7 Darrn Foard/Shutterstock.com; p. 9 EBFoto/Shutterstock.com; p. 11 Chase Clausen/Shutterstock.com; p. 13 Stephen N Haynes/Shutterstock.com; pp. 15, 24 (nest) Peter Dean/Shutterstock.com; pp. 17, 24 (fur) lexan/Shutterstock.com; p. 19 prochasson frederic/Shutterstock.com; p. 21 NguyenLuong Pictures/Shutterstock.com; p. 23 Abeselom Zerit/Shutterstock.com.

Printed in the United States of America

CPSIA compliance information: Batch #CS15GS: For further information contact Gareth Stevens, New York, New York at 1-800-542-2595.

Contents

Some gorillas live at the zoo.